Historical American Biographies

SOJOURNER TRUTH

Abolitionist and Women's Rights Activist

Catherine Bernard

Enslow Publishers, Inc.

40 Industrial Road   PO Box 38
Box 398   Aldershot
Berkeley Heights, NJ 07922 Hants GU12 6BP
USA   UK

http://www.enslow.com

For Mom, Dad, and Jeanne with love,
and for Peter, as always

Library of Congress Cataloging-in-Publication Data

Bernard, Catherine.
   Sojourner Truth : abolitionist and women's rights activist / Catherine Bernard.
     p. cm. — (Historical American biographies)
Includes bibliographical references (p.) and index.
  ISBN 0-7660-1257-3
  1. Truth, Sojourner, d. 1883—Juvenile literature. 2. Afro-American
abolitionists—Biography—Juvenile literature. 3. Afro-American
women—Biography—Juvenile literature. 4. Abolitionists—United States—
Biography—Juvenile literature. 5. Social reformers—United
States—Biography—Juvenile literature. [1. Truth, Sojourner, d. 1883.
2. Abolitionists. 3. Reformers. 4. Afro-Americans—Biography. 5. Women—
Biography.] I. Title. II. Series.
E185.97.T8 B44 2001
305.5'67'092—dc21

                               00-009279

Printed in the United States of America

10 9 8 7 6 5 4 3 2 1

To Our Readers: All Internet Addresses in this book were active and appropriate
at the time we went to press. Any comments or suggestions can be sent by e-mail
to Comments@enslow.com or to the address on the back cover.

Illustration Credits: Enslow Publishers, Inc., pp. 50, 77; From the
Collection of the New-York Historical Society, pp. 4, 34, 39; Library of
Congress, pp. 9, 17, 47, 49, 53, 58, 61, 67, 69, 74, 78, 80, 82, 84, 85,
87, 91, 97.

Cover Illustrations: Library of Congress.

CONTENTS

This illustration appeared at the beginning of Truth's 1851
Narrative of Sojourner Truth.

1

"AIN'T I A WOMAN?"

On May 29, 1851, Sojourner Truth stepped up to the podium. Hundreds of people were gathered in Akron, Ohio, that afternoon for the second day of the women's rights convention. People came from all over to discuss important women's rights issues, such as educational reform, equal job opportunities, and the right to vote.

Speakers had been on all day, but many guests were surprised when Truth stepped on stage. The reason was very simple—Truth was the *only* black person at the convention. The color of her skin would not stop her from speaking, however, or from being heard. The moment Truth began to speak, a hush fell over the crowd. No one could help but listen to her deep and powerful voice.[1]

Born a slave in New York in the late 1790s, Truth never learned to read or write. As a result, almost all of what is known of her life comes from other people's accounts of her. The famous story of the Akron speech, for example, was related twelve years later by the president of the convention, Frances Gage. Truth knew what was being written about her, though. She was an extremely savvy woman who understood the importance of having her name widely known. For Truth, Gage's publication of her story simply meant more publicity for her cause.[2] In fact, Gage's version of the speech became so well-known that it is part of the foundation of Sojourner Truth's legend.

By 1851, Truth had already spoken extensively in New York, Pennsylvania, New England, and the Midwest.[3] By 1878, she had lectured in a total of twenty-one states, plus the District of Columbia.[4] She spoke out against the oppression of slaves and women across the country. Truth was a freedom fighter in every sense of the phrase.

Truth was accustomed to standing out in the crowd. The convention in Akron was no different. Truth looked different from the other women in more ways than just the color of her skin. On that day, as usual, she wore a plain gray dress, a white turban, and an unfashionable sunbonnet. Her style of dress did not match the fashions of the middle-class and upper-class white women gathered at the convention. Truth did not mind, though. She was not there to be fashionable. She was there to spread her message.[5]

Despite her unusual appearance, people could not help but be drawn to Truth. Her speeches were always moving. They often drew heavily on her own experiences as a slave. A devout Christian, Truth used biblical parables and Christian hymns in her talks. Many of her stories were very funny and almost always a bit sarcastic. At the same time, however, Truth was an extremely kind person. She referred to her listeners as "honey" and "child," and adapted an almost grandmotherly tone when speaking. Truth was no ordinary speaker. Even her adversaries were captivated by her unique style.

According to Gage, there were many who opposed the idea of Truth's speaking at Akron that day and making the convention an "abolition affair." Abolition was a movement to do away with slavery in the United States. Some of the women in Akron thought allowing an ex-slave and abolitionist such as Truth to speak might take attention away from women's rights issues. They begged Gage not to allow Truth to speak. To these objections, Gage simply answered, "We shall see when the time comes."[6]

Despite thoughts that abolition was not related to the women's rights movement, the two issues actually had much in common. One of the most ideal locations for these debates was the very state Truth was visiting—Ohio. Ohio was a free state, meaning it had outlawed slavery. It was also known as a "border state," because only the Ohio River separated it from the slaveholding state of Kentucky. For this reason, many runaway slaves tried to escape to Ohio. As a result, people of the state were often divided in their views on slavery, and they held many debates as to how strict Ohio's fugitive slave laws should be.[7]

In 1850, proslavery Americans won a major battle with the passage of a stricter fugitive slave law. This law made it a federal crime to help escaped slaves. It also gave slave owners the right to recapture slaves. Despite these laws, many abolitionists risked their lives to help slaves escape. Through a complex web of secret trails known as the Underground Railroad, many slaves found their way to freedom in the North. Between 1830 and 1850, conductors of this secret network helped thousands of slaves escape to freedom nationwide.

Soon people began to realize that many of the issues of freedom being raised about slaves also pertained to women. Women and blacks were fighting for many of the same basic human rights. As abolitionism grew in Ohio and across the Northern half of the country, so did the women's rights movement.

This famous drawing was used by abolitionists to protest the Fugitive Slave Law. It shows slaves being violently seized by trackers.

In the midst of all these events was Sojourner Truth. On the first day of the convention, she quietly listened to the other lecturers. During intermissions she sold copies of her book, *The Narrative of Sojourner Truth*, which she published herself. Although Truth never learned to read or write, she had friends help her record the experiences of her life so that she could publish an autobiography. Because she was not as well-known as other abolitionists of the time, Truth sold her books at various conventions in order to make a living. Her sales in Akron that May were fairly successful.

According to Gage, there was a bit more excitement at the convention on the second day. Several of the men in the audience began making comments about what a real woman was. They argued that women were naturally weaker than men. They thought women needed help to do such simple activities as climbing in and out of carriages and walking over ditches. Some also brought up the issue of slavery, saying that whites were naturally the dominant race. When Truth heard these prejudiced comments against her gender and her race, she could no longer keep silent. She walked to the podium and began to speak in a voice that sounded "like rolling thunder":

> Nobody eber help me into carriages, or ober mud puddles, or gives me any best place . . . and ar'n't I a woman? Look at me! Look at my arm! . . . I have plowed and planted, and gathered into barns, and no man could head [beat] me—and ar'n't I a woman? I could work as much and eat as much as a man (when I could get it), and bear the lash as well—and ar'n't I a woman? I have borne thirteen chilern and seen 'em mos' all sold off into slavery, and when I cried out with a mother's grief, none but Jesus heard—and ain't I a woman?[8]

Gage's version of the speech exaggerated some aspects of Truth's life. For example, Truth had only five children, not thirteen. Also, Gage's version of Truth's speech was written in a stilted Southern dialect. Truth never lived in the South, and therefore, did not speak in such a manner. Gage probably wrote it in this way so that people would believe they were actually the words of an ex-slave, rather than a white abolitionist. In fact, many recent historians have argued convincingly that Gage edited most of Truth's speech to make it more dramatic. Most likely, it was Gage, not Truth, who coined the famous phrase, "Ain't I a woman?" Regardless of the precise words and the exaggeration of detail, though, the message was still clearly Sojourner Truth's.

Truth's message was historic because of the way she combined the issues of slavery and women's rights. She gave a new definition of womanhood in the nineteenth century. Truth's woman was not a helpless creature. She was strong, independent, and capable of doing anything as well as a man—much like Truth herself. Truth also spoke out against slavery. Mentioning her labor, her beatings, and her children being sold was her way of highlighting the evils of slavery. More than anything, though, Truth demonstrated her own strength, her fierce sense of independence, and her iron will. She would not let anyone tell her she was an inferior human being because she happened to be a black woman. Despite the many hardships she faced during her lifetime, Truth not only survived, she overcame.

Her story is truly an inspiring one. Sojourner Truth beat every odd against her to become a powerful and influential voice for social reform in nineteenth-century America. And she accomplished it all, simply because she knew she could.

2

A SLAVE
NAMED
ISABELLA

Sojourner Truth was born a slave in Hurley, New York, sometime around 1797. No one knows the exact date because slaves' birthdays were considered unimportant. Back then, she was called Isabella. She would not change her name to Sojourner Truth until much later in life. Isabella had no last name. As a slave, it was only important to know that she belonged to her master. At birth, Isabella was the property of Colonel Johannes Hardenbergh.

Colonel Hardenbergh owned a large estate in the rural town of Hurley, in Ulster County, New York. His Dutch ancestors had been some of the town's earliest settlers. He was one of the richest men in the county and owned about six or seven slaves.[1] Colonel Hardenbergh spoke English as well as a language called Low Dutch. He taught his slaves only Dutch—it was easier to control them if they could not communicate with anyone outside the estate.[2]

Family

Isabella was somewhat lucky. Both of her parents, James and Elizabeth, were also owned by Colonel Hardenbergh. Many slaves were sold to different owners and never got to know their families. Her father was very tall, straight, and strong. He was called Baumfree, which is a Dutch word that means tree. Elizabeth was known as Mau-Mau Bett. She was Baumfree's third wife. His previous two wives had been sold away.

Baumfree and Mau-Mau had between ten and twelve children. All but two of them were sold to different farms. Isabella and her brother Peter got to stay at the Hardenbergh estate. Because so many of her children were gone, Mau-Mau was often very sad. Sometimes Isabella would find her crying. When Isabella asked her mother what was wrong, she would say, "Oh my child, I am thinking of your brothers and sisters that have been taken away from me."[3] Mau-Mau constantly worried about the possibility of Peter and Isabella being taken away as well. Mau-Mau would often tell Isabella the story of her two older siblings to explain the pain and fear with which she lived.

One snowy morning, Mau-Mau's five-year-old son, Michael, went to gather some firewood. In the meantime, a sleigh arrived at the estate. At first, the innocent child was delighted to see such a new sight. As he watched a strange man place his little sister Nancy on the sleigh, however, Michael began to get confused. His confusion soon turned to horror as he then saw the man shove Nancy into a small box, shut the lid, and lock it. Michael tried to run away but was quickly caught and secured on the sleigh. Little Michael and Nancy had been sold. They would never see their parents again. Baumfree and Mau-Mau could do nothing but watch helplessly as their children were stolen away from them.[4]

One of Mau-Mau's few comforts was her strong belief in God. After Mau-Mau's work was done for the day, she would gather her children and teach them her religious beliefs. Mau-Mau told her children that they could ask God for help whenever they fell into trouble.[5] Isabella took these teachings very seriously and held them sacred her entire life.

Inherited Property

Isabella never knew Colonel Hardenbergh very well because he died when she was very young. His estate was left to his son, Charles. Slaves were considered part of the estate, so they, too, were

How Truth Learned the Bible

Truth never learned to read or write, but she learned scriptures by heart by having them read to her. She did not like adults to read to her, however, because they often added their own commentary. "Children," Truth said, "would re-read the same sentence to her, as often as she wished, and without comment; and in that way, she was enabled to see what her own mind could make of the record . . . and not what others thought it to mean."[6]

inherited by Charles Hardenbergh. Hardenbergh decided to move his newly acquired slaves and livestock to a house he had built nearby.

With no slave quarters at his mansion, the slaves were forced to sleep in the cellar. All the slaves, both male and female, slept in the same room. There was no privacy. Each slave got only a little straw and a blanket as a bed. The one room was very dark and damp. Sometimes, a hard rain would turn the dirt floor to mud. As a result of living in these conditions, many of the slaves were often sick.

In 1808, Isabella's second master became very ill. It was clear that he was dying. The slaves began to worry about what would happen to them after Charles Hardenbergh died. A few days later, they got their answer. After Charles Hardenbergh's funeral, his entire estate, including his slaves, was auctioned off. Nine-year-old Isabella would be separated from her beloved family.

By the time Charles Hardenbergh died, Baumfree was already very old. His arms and legs had become disfigured as a result of his years of labor and living in the damp cellar. The Hardenbergh family knew they would get no money for him if they sent him to auction. Essentially, he was valueless and useless to them, so they freed him.

In New York State, it was illegal to free slaves like Baumfree, who were no longer productive and had no means of fending for themselves. In an attempt to satisfy the law, the Hardenberghs also freed Mau-Mau, who, in theory, could take care of her husband. While Mau-Mau was certainly younger than Baumfree, it was still nearly impossible for her to provide for them both. Neither could speak English, nor did they have a way of earning a living in the outside world. The Hardenberghs told them they could continue living in the cellar if Mau-Mau agreed to continue working for the family. They had no choice but to accept.

A New Master

Meanwhile, Isabella and her brother Peter were put on the auction block. Isabella watched in horrified silence as Peter was sold to a man who lived very far away. Then it was her turn. At first, no one bid on

An advertisement for an upcoming slave auction.

Isabella. The auctioneer decided to throw in a flock of sheep to sweeten the deal. A man named John Nealy could not pass up such a bargain, so he bought Isabella and the sheep for a mere one hundred dollars.[7]

Nealy was a shopkeeper who also lived in Ulster County. He and his wife had recently moved from Massachusetts to New York. They did not get along well with the surrounding Dutch community. Perhaps this was because the Nealys only spoke English, while their neighbors mainly spoke Dutch. For Isabella, of course, the language barrier was a problem. How could she be expected to understand her English-speaking masters if she only knew Dutch?

Nealy's wife tried to teach young Isabella English, but she was a very impatient woman. Although Isabella tried to learn, it was never fast enough for her mistress. Mrs. Nealy would always end up screaming at the child or throwing things at her. At times, Mrs. Nealy would turn her husband against Isabella. The most memorable and painful instance was a day when Nealy used a burning hot rod to beat Isabella. The scars from that torturous beating stayed with her for the rest of her life.[8]

Even though she had been there less than a year, Isabella hated life at the Nealys' and she prayed to be rescued.[9] One winter day, after many weeks of waiting, Isabella's prayers were answered when her father came to visit her. At first, she could not tell him of her misery for fear they might be overheard. As Baumfree prepared to leave, Isabella walked him to the gate. She told him of her horrible mistress and showed him the scars on her back. He was horrified and promised to try to help his daughter.

Baumfree thought he could try to find a new master for Isabella, since slaves were sometimes able to help one another by finding out who the kinder masters were and then convincing them to buy their friends and family. Not long after seeing her father, Isabella learned that this was precisely what he had done for her.

Somehow, Baumfree convinced a fisherman named Martin Schriver to inquire about Isabella. Schriver lived about five miles from the Nealys. He came to their farm to ask Isabella if she would like to work for him instead. Isabella quickly agreed. She figured nothing could be worse than the Nealys. Schriver bought Isabella for $105.[10] Baumfree had kept his promise by rescuing his daughter from the awful Nealys.

Another Master

Life with the Schrivers was not as hard for Isabella. She spent many days outdoors, gardening, carrying fish, and even shopping at the local market. The Schrivers were not cruel like the Nealys and they did not beat Isabella. They also spoke both English and Dutch, so it was much easier for Isabella to understand them. Since no one was constantly yelling at her, Isabella was not under pressure to learn English and quickly picked up the language. In fact, Isabella learned it so well, she also picked up the bad habit of mildly cursing from time to time!

While working for the Schrivers, Isabella received some painful news. Her mother, Mau-Mau, had died. Baumfree had come home one winter morning to find his wife lying on the floor. A few hours later, she died. It had simply been too cold in the cellar for the woman to live. Baumfree was overcome with grief. Isabella worried about how he would survive without his wife. A short time later, Isabella's worries were over. Baumfree, too, passed away. Without anyone to help take care of him, he had starved to death.[11]

Around the same time, a stranger visited the Schrivers' farm. His name was John Dumont. He

Truth's Bad Habit

As a child at the Schrivers', Truth began smoking a pipe. One time, she was criticized for her bad habit when a friend told her that "the Bible tells us that no unclean thing can enter the Kingdom of Heaven." Truth wryly replied, "True, but when I go to Heaven I expect to leave my breath behind me."[12] Truth eventually did quit smoking for health reasons in 1868.

was a farmer from New Paltz, New York. He offered to buy tall, strong Isabella from the Schrivers. For the third and last time in the thirteen-year-old's life, Isabella was sold. This time she was sold for about $175.[13]

Isabella's Last Master

Dumont was a fairly good man, as far as slave owners went. He was not excessively cruel like the Nealys, but he did beat Isabella. Still, Isabella was always very eager to please him. Dumont could not help but notice Isabella's hard work. He often bragged about Isabella, saying, she "is better to me than a *man*—for she will do a good family's washing in the night, and be ready in the morning to go into the field, where she will do as much at raking and binding as my best hands."[14]

While Isabella's ambition pleased her master, it was not looked upon so kindly by the other slaves. They could not understand how she could be so eager to please a man who kept her in captivity. Also, the older slaves could not keep up with the young Isabella. Many were resentful of her for making them look bad, even if she did it unintentionally.[15]

Another person on the estate who was not happy with Isabella was Dumont's wife, Sally. Much like Mrs. Nealy, Mrs. Dumont was never satisfied with anything Isabella did and constantly yelled at her. While Mr. Dumont praised Isabella for the amount of work she did, Mrs. Dumont accused her of doing her jobs only half way. In 1812, though, these accusations proved false. In an incident involving a white servant girl named Kate and the Dumonts' ten-year-old daughter, Gertrude, Isabella proved Mrs. Dumont wrong.

One of Isabella's chores was to wash potatoes in the morning and boil them for breakfast. Isabella would scrub the potatoes as hard as she could in order to make certain that not one speck of dirt remained on them. Yet, somehow, there always remained an unusually large amount of dirt in the bottom of the pot of water. Isabella knew she had thoroughly cleaned the potatoes and could not understand how they could still be dirty. When Mrs. Dumont scolded Isabella for her carelessness, Gertrude defended her. Isabella was both surprised and happy to hear the Dumonts' daughter speak up for her. Together, the two young girls plotted to unravel the mystery of the dirty potatoes.

The next day, Isabella cleaned the potatoes and put them in the pot as usual. While Isabella went to milk the cows, Gertrude hid in the kitchen. As soon as Isabella left, the servant, Kate, came in and dumped ashes into the water. Gertrude ran off to tell her father what had really been happening to the potatoes. With the help of her new friend, Isabella was able to clear her name.[16]

3

FREEDOM

When Isabella was about sixteen years old, she met and fell in love with a man named Robert, a slave from a neighboring farm. Robert's master, Mr. Catlin, did not approve of the relationship. He wanted Robert to marry one of his own slaves. That way, any children they had would become Catlin's property. In other words, Catlin, like most masters, hoped to "breed" his own slaves.

Even though Catlin forbade Robert from seeing Isabella, the young man still visited her. One day, Catlin and his son discovered that Robert was missing and tracked him to the Dumonts' so they might catch him visiting Isabella. When they found him, they began to beat him horribly for his disobedience. As Robert lay on the ground bleeding, it looked like he might not live if they continued to hit and kick him.

Dumont intervened, telling Catlin and his son that he would have no slaves killed on his property. The two men stopped and prepared to take Robert home, but Dumont followed them back to their farm to make sure they did not kill him on the way. Although Dumont had helped prevent Robert's murder that day, it was still the last day Isabella ever saw him.[1]

Marriage and Family

Soon after the incident with Robert, Dumont forced Isabella to marry one of his slaves, Thomas. Like Isabella's father, her new husband had had two wives before her. Between about 1815 and 1826, Isabella had five children with Thomas—Diana, Peter, Elizabeth, Sophia, and Thomas. Isabella was happy to be a mother, even though it was hard work. Since she was, of course, still expected to work in the fields, Isabella would put an infant in a basket and tie it securely to a tree branch. With this makeshift hammock, Isabella was able to watch and rock her child while continuing to work.[2]

Freedom

During this time in Isabella's life, there was much happening to New York State's slavery laws. Many states in the North were passing laws to end slavery. Unlike the South, which needed slaves to work its huge cotton and tobacco plantations, most farmers in the North had small farms where they grew just enough for themselves and their families. The North was also developing an economy based on trade and industry, rather than agriculture alone. For these reasons, and because the North had thousands of immigrants arriving each year to work in the cities, slaveholders' excuses for upholding slavery were no longer valid. So Northern states were taking steps to get rid of it entirely.

According to the New York state legislature, all slaves born after July 4, 1799, were "free." However, they had to remain as unpaid servants until the age of twenty-nine for boys, and twenty-four for girls.[3] Because Isabella was born before 1799, only her children fell within the law. In 1817, all that changed. Under a new law passed by New York State, all slaves over the age of twenty-eight were to be freed by July 4, 1827. For Isabella, this new law meant that she would be a free woman in ten more years.

When Dumont heard about the law, he decided to do even more for Isabella, as a reward for her years of hard work. Dumont promised Isabella that he would free her one year early if she continued to work hard. So she worked twice as hard in order to earn her early emancipation. In the process, Isabella severely hurt her right hand. At times, her injury made it painful and difficult to work. Even this hardship did not keep Isabella from trying her best, because she wanted so much to be free.

Finally, July 4, 1826, came. Isabella went to her master to remind him of his promise. To Isabella's surprise, Dumont refused to free her. He claimed that she had not worked hard enough as a result of her injured hand.

Isabella was very angry. She had always done her best for Dumont and now he was pretending otherwise. With typical determination, she decided to hold Dumont to his promise. Isabella worked hard for Dumont all during the summer of 1826 and even into the fall harvest season. Despite her anger, she did not want to leave him short-handed during the farm's busiest season.

One night in late fall 1826, Isabella felt she heard the voice of God telling her what to do. She bundled up only her infant daughter, Sophia, and packed up some food. With nothing else, Isabella left the Dumont estate and literally walked to freedom.

After walking for five miles, she ended up at the home of Levi Rowe, a kind man Isabella had known for several years. Rowe was very sick and could not help Isabella and her child himself. Instead, he told her to go to his friends, Isaac and Maria VanWagener. The VanWageners were members of a local Dutch Reformed Church, and they strongly opposed slavery. When Isabella arrived at their house and told them her story, they welcomed her into their home.

The next day, Dumont came looking for Isabella. When he found her at the VanWageners', he demanded that she return, but Isabella refused. Although the VanWageners opposed slavery, they wanted to avoid an unpleasant confrontation. They offered Dumont $25 for Isabella and her child. Dumont accepted.[4]

After Dumont left, Isabella thanked Mr. VanWagener, mistakenly thinking he was her new master. To this he replied, "there is but *one* master; and he who is your master is *my* master."[5] Isabella understood the religious meaning of his statement right away. Mr. VanWagener was telling Isabella that her only master was God. On hearing these words, Isabella realized that, for the first time in her life, she was free.

Searching for a Lost Son

Isabella decided to stay and work for the VanWageners. Her life there was very satisfying, and she even took VanWagener for her last name. In a short time, however, Isabella discovered that her problems were far from over.

Before Isabella had left Dumont, her master had sold her son, Peter. At the VanWageners', Isabella received the troublesome news that her son had

John Dumont

The last episode from the first edition of Truth's *Narrative* is not directly about her, but rather about the conversion of her old master, John Dumont. While visiting her daughter Diana in the spring of 1849, Truth stopped to speak with her old master. She was delighted to hear that, after many years, he had come to realize that slavery was evil. Dumont told Truth that "slavery was the wickedest thing in the world, the greatest curse the earth had ever felt—that it was then very clear to his mind that it was so, though, while he was a slaveholder himself, he did not see it so."[6]

then been illegally sold south. Peter had originally been bought by a man named Dr. Gedney, who wanted to take him to England as a servant. After deciding Peter was too young to travel overseas, Dr. Gedney sold the boy to his brother Solomon. Solomon Gedney, in turn, broke New York state law by selling Peter to a farmer in Alabama named Fowler. Although slavery had been abolished in the North, it was still legal in the South. This meant that Peter might never be freed. As long as he was trapped in Alabama, he was in grave danger. Isabella was worried for the safety and future of her son, but she did not feel defeated.[7]

Isabella returned to the Dumonts'. She confronted her old master and mistress and demanded to know what had happened to her son. Mr. Dumont denied knowing anything about Gedney's actions. Mrs. Dumont laughed at Isabella for making such a fuss over a little black boy. Isabella started to leave, but then stopped. She turned and said in a very slow and determined manner, "I have no money, but God has enough, or what's better! And I'll have my child again." In later remembering that day, Isabella said, "Oh my God! I know'd I'd have him agin. I was sure God would help me to get him. Why, I felt so *tall within*—I felt as if the *power of a nation* was with me!"[8]

Next, Isabella went to Mrs. Gedney, the mother of the man who had sold Peter to Fowler. Mrs. Gedney was just as unsympathetic as Mrs. Dumont had been. Mrs. Gedney's daughter Eliza was also in Alabama, and she complained to Isabella that she missed her child just as much as Isabella missed hers. Isabella realized it was useless trying to talk to this woman. Before she left, Isabella pointed out that, while Eliza was in Alabama, she was free. Peter had been dragged illegally against his will, and was in danger of remaining a slave for the rest of his life.[9]

Determined as ever, Isabella returned to the VanWageners for help. They sent her to the nearby town of Kingston. Once in Kingston, Isabella met some Quaker abolitionists who offered to help.

Quakers were members of a branch of Christianity that strongly opposed slavery. They told her how to find the county courthouse and suggested that she file a complaint against Gedney. They also helped Isabella pay her legal fees.

Isabella filed a complaint against Solomon Gedney for unlawfully taking her son south. The case was brought before a grand jury. Surprisingly, the jury decided in her favor, even though she was a black woman bringing suit against a white man—a rare occurrence at that time. After many legal complications, papers were finally served to Gedney, ordering him to return Peter.

At first, Peter did not want to go back to his mother. Peter was now legally free, but because he had been separated from her for over a year, he was confused about where he belonged. After a little while, Isabella was able to convince him that she was his mother and he belonged with her.

Once Peter agreed, Isabella was able to get her first good look at her son. She was horrified to discover that Peter was scarred from head to toe. Fowler had repeatedly whipped, kicked, and beaten Peter until his tiny body was virtually maimed as a result. Although Isabella knew there was nothing she could do about the old scars, she knew that Peter would never be beaten like that again. Isabella thanked God for returning her son and swore that no child of hers would ever be taken away again.[10]

Isabella was so happy to have her son back that she did not grasp the full magnitude of what she had just achieved. In her fight to win back her child, Isabella had become one of the first blacks in the country to sue a white person successfully. For the first, but certainly not the last, time, Isabella had made history.

4

ISABELLA IN THE CITY

After rescuing her son, Isabella and Peter lived with the VanWageners, while Isabella continued to earn a living doing housework in the Kingston area. Although she was content, she missed her other children, who were still slaves at the Dumonts'. Once the lawsuit ended, Isabella reestablished contact with her old master. Since the two were once again on good terms, Isabella was allowed to visit her daughters on the estate.

During this time, Isabella became very serious about the Methodist religion. She always attended church services and meetings. It was at one of these meetings that Isabella met a woman named Miss

Grear in 1828. The white school teacher from New York grew fond of Isabella and especially of young Peter. Grear was on her way back to New York City and suggested that Isabella and her son join her. In New York, there would be more educational opportunities for Peter, and Grear could help Isabella find a better housekeeping job with a family she knew.[1] In addition, there were many other free blacks in the city—a prospect that appealed to Isabella.

While thinking about the possible move, Isabella considered what reasons she might have to stay. To begin with, she did not have to worry about her husband. Thomas had been freed on July 4, 1827. Like Isabella, he worked wherever he could find jobs, but times were harder on Thomas than on Isabella. He never made enough money to survive and he died in debt less than a year after his emancipation.[2] As for their children, all but Peter were still slaves at the Dumonts'. They were fairly well taken care of there, but they would not be freed for several years, until each turned twenty-four.

After taking all these facts into consideration, Isabella decided it would be better for her and Peter to go. Peter had been getting into trouble lately, lying and even stealing. New York City would give them a fresh start, away from the environment where slavery had plagued both their lives.

New York City

Life in the city was dramatically different from the country life of Ulster County. Instead of sprawling farms, Isabella saw tightly packed buildings lining cobblestone streets. The streets were crowded with horse-drawn carriages and people constantly moving. New York was certainly not a city that ever stood still! The unfamiliar sights and sounds must have been somewhat confusing and even frightening for newcomers. After a time, though, Isabella became

A view of New York City as it appeared in the mid-nineteenth century when Isabella moved there.

accustomed to New York and learned to navigate the busy streets along with everyone else.

Grear helped Isabella find work as a servant in the homes of some family and friends. After finding a job and a place to live, the next important task for Isabella was to find a church in the big city. At first, she attended the John Street Church, a Methodist congregation. She did not feel comfortable there, though, mainly because services were segregated. She soon changed to the Mother Zion African Methodist Episcopal (AME) Church. The AME Church had an all-black congregation and Isabella felt at home there. In fact, the church would prove to be more like a home than Isabella could possibly imagine.

Family Reunions and the Church

When Isabella was still in Ulster County, she had established contact with her sister Sophia, who lived in New York. After her move, Isabella and her sister got to meet face-to-face in New York. Sophia told Isabella that their brother Michael was also living in the city. Isabella had never met Michael, but she remembered her mother's story about him and their sister. During their first meeting, Isabella anxiously asked about Nancy, Mau-Mau's other child who had been carried away in the sleigh. Michael gave Isabella the sad news that Nancy had been living in New York but had passed away a few months earlier. Michael described her and mentioned that she had been a member of the AME Church as well. As Michael spoke of Nancy, Isabella realized she had met her at church without even knowing who she was. Isabella remembered being "struck with the peculiar feeling of her hand—the bony hardness so just like mine? and yet I could not know she was my sister; and now I see she looked *so* like my mother." Isabella, Sophia, and Michael wept, and Isabella wondered to herself "what is this slavery, that it can do such dreadful things."[3]

Through people she knew at church, Isabella became a volunteer at the Magdelene House of Refuge—a shelter for homeless women, run by a man named Elijah Pierson. Isabella came to know Pierson through his black servant, Katy. Eventually, Isabella took over the housekeeping position when Katy left to visit her children. Pierson was not just Isabella's employer, he was also a kind of religious mentor. Many of Pierson's religious views were similar to Isabella's, so she found it easy to follow his leadership. Unfortunately for Isabella, though, Pierson eventually became extremely fanatical about his religion. He even began telling people that he was a prophet of God.

While Isabella was working at Pierson's one day, a stranger came to the door. He was a striking man with long hair, a beard, and piercing eyes.[4] Isabella's early impression was that this man might be Jesus Christ himself. Actually, it was a con artist named

Robert Matthews. This man went by the name Matthias, and he would change Isabella's life forever.

The Kingdom of Matthias

Together, Pierson and Matthias formed their own religious "community." They called it the Kingdom. The Kingdom advocated equality for all, regardless of race, sex, class, or age, and proclaimed that "our creed is truth."[5] Despite warnings from family and friends that Matthias was an imposter, Isabella was attracted by the idea of his Kingdom. She agreed to join the community, along with several other very religious Methodists. She willingly gave Matthias her hard-earned money as well. The group brought all their possessions together and moved to a communal house in Sing Sing, New York.

Isabella thought she would be an equal in this community, despite being the only black person. Nonetheless, she always ended up doing most of the cooking and cleaning. In addition, she was often asked to leave the room when important decisions were being made.[6] Unfortunately for Isabella, these problems were minor compared to other happenings in the community.

Matthias now proclaimed himself to be Jesus personified, and Pierson claimed to be John the Baptist. Although the Kingdom was supposedly based on equality, Matthias was clearly in charge. He made all the decisions for the Kingdom and instituted such strange policies as communal bathing and free love. In addition, Matthias had control over all the finances of the Kingdom.[7] The community members were asked to give all their worldly possessions to the Kingdom. Isabella herself continued to give all the money she had, plus several pieces of furniture. Matthias must have used most of the money on himself—he was always dressed in fine clothing and his table was always spread with wonderful foods.[8]

Controversy in the Kingdom continued when Pierson mysteriously died in 1834. The circumstances surrounding his death became even more bizarre when Matthias was accused of poisoning him. As if that were not enough, two members of the Kingdom, Ann and Benjamin Folger, accused Isabella of witchcraft, as well as of trying to poison them. The Kingdom of Matthias was collapsing and it seemed Isabella was going down with it.

As usual, Isabella would not give up without a fight. She once again turned to the courts to help with her problems. Isabella sued the Folgers for their slander—making false accusations that ruined her good name. For a second time, Isabella eventually won a lawsuit against white people. She was awarded a small amount of money for the Folgers' lies. Isabella also agreed to tell her side of the story to a reporter named Gilbert Vale. In 1835, Vale published a book entitled *Fanaticism, Its Sources and Influence*, in order to help Isabella clear her name.[9]

Matthias was also eventually acquitted of Pierson's murder. Exposed as an imposter, he moved out west and died alone six years later.

Trouble With Peter

As a result of her involvement with the Kingdom and the lawsuit, Isabella had not been able to keep a careful eye on Peter. During her absence, her teenage son had dropped out of school and started hanging out with a group of dangerous troublemakers. Isabella tried to discipline him upon her return but had little success. Peter continually wound up in jail and his mother would always bail him out.

Finally, Isabella warned her son that she would no longer help him if he continued to get into trouble. Peter did not believe his mother until he was once again thrown in jail for theft.

Robert Matthias convinced many people, including Isabella, that he was a prophet. This pamphlet discussed Matthias's trial for fraudulent behavior.

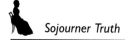

This time, Isabella refused to help. Though it pained her to do so, she felt it was in his best interest.

Peter was a clever boy, and although he was trapped in jail, he quickly thought of a plan of action. Peter often used the alias Peter Williams when he committed crimes. Since he was already stuck in jail, he decided to send for the *real* Peter Williams to ask for help. Williams was a respectable New York businessman. Surprisingly, he agreed to come to Peter's aid.

Williams's help was not necessarily free, however. He told Peter he would help on the condition that Peter clean up his act and leave New York. Peter agreed. The next day, Williams helped Peter get a job aboard a whaling ship. At that time, working aboard a ship was considered a means of disciplining unruly young men. Peter left in the summer of 1839. Isabella did not hear from him until the fall of the following year, when she received the following letter, dated October 17, 1840:

> My Dear Beloved Mother:
>
> I take this opportunity to write to you and inform you that I am well, and in hopes for to find you the same. I am got on board the same unlucky ship Done, of Nantucket. I am sorry for to say, that I have been punished once severely. . . . We have had bad luck, but in hopes to have better. . . . Mother, I hope you do not forget me. . . . I hope you all will forgive me for all that I have done.
>
> Your son,
> PETER VAN WAGENER[10]

Touched by her son's letter, Isabella dictated a letter back almost immediately. The two kept in contact until September 1841, when Isabella received a fifth and final letter from her son. After that date, Isabella never heard from or about Peter again.[11]

A Change of Life

By the early 1840s, Isabella was very disappointed with life in New York City. The Matthias scandal had humiliated her and the loss of her son had left her heartbroken. Conditions in New York were also very poor for free blacks. Isabella realized that she had been working for nearly seven years since she had given her money to Matthias, yet still had virtually

Looking for a Place to Stay

Isabella left New York without any idea where she was going or where she would sleep at night. In her *Narrative*, she recounted wandering from inn to inn, asking if she might stay the night, and always receiving a negative answer. Finally, she came to a large building that "was occupied as court-house, tavern, and jail." She was told she could stay, provided she did not mind being locked into one of the unoccupied cells. Tired as she was, she refused without a second thought. She continued on her way, "preferring to walk beneath the open sky, to being locked up by a stranger in such a place."[12]

nothing to show for it. She came to the sad conclusion that New York was a place where "the rich rob the poor, and the poor rob one another," so she decided to leave.[13]

On the morning of June 1, 1843, Isabella later said, she felt the voice of God telling her to travel and spread his word.[14] The woman who left that morning decided that the slave name Isabella was no longer acceptable for one of God's free pilgrims. Considering the nature of her journey, she decided on Sojourner, a synonym for traveler. For a last name, she eventually chose "Truth," probably as a reminder of the quest for truth that would guide the rest of her life. On June 1, 1843, Sojourner Truth began her journey.

5

ABOLITION

S ojourner Truth spent many months traveling in the northeastern United States after leaving New York City. For the most part, she visited various religious meetings.

In mid-nineteenth-century America, there was a large religious revival among Protestant churches, particularly Methodists, which became known as the Second Great Awakening. As part of this movement, people would reaffirm their own religious beliefs and try to convert others. In the 1840s, it became very popular for groups of people to gather and camp in wagons and tents to pray and to listen to religious lecturers. These religious camp meetings gave Truth her first taste of speaking in front of groups. With very little hesitation, she would get up in front of large crowds and preach about God and religion. Later in life, Truth would begin to incorporate stories about her life as a slave as well.

Lecturer

Truth was an impressive figure even before she began her moving speeches. Once she started to lecture, the crowd would be entranced by the woman and her stories. At times, she would make them laugh with her sarcastic sense of humor. Other times, she would bring the crowd to tears with her stories about slavery. Truth also made certain to include in her lectures hymns that she had written herself. As a result of her unique style and unwavering faith, she became a favorite at many camp meetings.[1] She was often invited to come back and was recommended to speak at other meetings. In fact, Truth was so popular that she was able to make a living by speaking at meetings.

Truth was usually the only black person at these meetings, a fact that did not bother her. Once in a while, though, Truth feared for her safety. On one occasion, a group of rowdy young men was disturbing a camp meeting by rudely interrupting speakers while they preached. At first, Truth ran to hide, thinking they might attack her for being black. After stopping a moment, Truth changed her mind. "Shall

I run away and hide from the Devil?" she thought. "Have I not faith enough to go out and quell [quiet] that mob? . . . I'll go to the rescue, and the Lord shall go with and protect me."[2]

With that simple thought, Truth came out from her hiding place and began to sing in her loudest voice. The young men rushed toward her. Truth stopped her singing and asked why they wanted to hurt her. They replied that they did not want to hurt her, but rather, wanted to hear more of her stories and singing. Truth consented, so long as the young men would leave peacefully when she was done. They agreed and eventually left quietly. True to her word, Truth had calmed the crowd.[3]

The Northampton Association

Truth's travels led her to Springfield, Massachusetts, where she was once again involved with religious camp meetings. In Springfield, some friends of Truth's suggested that she go live at the Northampton Association of Education and Industry in Northampton, Massachusetts.[4] The Northampton Association was a cooperative farm where members worked together to produce silk from silkworms.

Unlike Matthias's Kingdom, the community at Northampton was truly a cooperative one. The founders insisted "that every laborer be a partner in the enterprise, filled with the spirit of ownership and participation."[5] This emphasis on equality was important in all aspects of the Northampton Association, and the community soon became well-known for its tolerance of all people, regardless of race, gender, religion, or class. It also happened to be one of the country's foremost centers for the abolition movement. At the Northampton Association, Truth finally found a community that promoted human equality.

Ironically, Truth was not very taken with life in Northampton at first glance. She came to Northampton during a dreary winter at the farm's beginnings, when "appearances did not correspond with the ideas of associationists."[6] While the appearance may not have appealed to Truth, the company she kept there certainly did. In fact, it would have been difficult for Truth not to have been impressed, considering that some of the most prominent abolitionists and intellectuals of the time visited or lived at Northampton.

Meeting Famous Abolitionists

Among the abolitionists visiting Northampton was the famous William Lloyd Garrison. Garrison had become involved in the abolition movement at a young age. In 1831, when he was only twenty-six years old, he launched *The Liberator*, one of the most influential antislavery newspapers in the country. In addition to editing *The Liberator*, Garrison was cofounder and president of the American Anti-Slavery

THE LIBERATOR.

VOL. I.]   WILLIAM LLOYD GARRISON AND ISAAC KNAPP, PUBLISHERS.   [NO. 33.

Boston, Massachusetts.]   OUR COUNTRY IS THE WORLD—OUR COUNTRYMEN ARE MANKIND.   [Saturday, August 13, 1831.

The Liberator, *edited by William Lloyd Garrison, was one of the most famous and influential antislavery publications of its time.*

Society, which worked to eliminate slavery in the United States.

In this setting, Truth was not the only black person living on the farm. Another black resident was David Ruggles, who was born free in Connecticut but had dedicated his life to the abolition movement. He contributed publicly by writing for an antislavery journal called *The Mirror of Liberty*. But it was Ruggles's underground contribution that directly helped slaves. Ruggles was the secretary of the New York Vigilance Committee—a secret organization that helped hundreds of runaway slaves escape from the South to freedom in the North.

Ruggles's position as a conductor of the Underground Railroad put him in personal danger, especially after passage of new fugitive slave laws. In 1793, Congress passed the Fugitive Slave Act, which allowed slaveholders to recapture runaway slaves. The law also said that people helping runaways were subject to a fine. Before 1850, however, this law was more or less ignored by abolitionists, and thousands of slaves were able to escape through the work of the Underground Railroad.

After 1850, helping escaped slaves became a much more dangerous activity with the passage of a stricter Fugitive Slave Act. The law was passed as part of the famous Compromise of 1850. In order to satisfy both antislavery Northerners and slave-holding Southerners, Congress agreed to admit California to the Union as a free state in order to make Northerners happy, but also agreed to update the 1793 Fugitive Slave Act for Southerners. This

Harriet Tubman, the Moses of her People
Another famous conductor of the Underground Railroad was Harriet Tubman. She was born a slave in Maryland but escaped to the North in 1849. She made many trips back to the South, helping close to three hundred slaves escape. Tubman even used her own house in Auburn, New York, as a station on the escape route. Because of her work in freeing slaves from bondage, she became known as the Moses of her people, after the biblical hero who freed the Jews from bondage in Egypt.

Harriet Tubman was known as the Moses of her people because she helped free so many slaves through the Underground Railroad.

Most fugitives on the Underground Railroad traveled to the Northern states or to Canada, but some fled to Florida, Mexico, and the Caribbean.

new law increased controversy between the North and the South. Many Northerners did not want any part of supporting slavery, nor did they agree with the severity of the new law. The new law stated that a person only had to match a description of a runaway slave for a federal marshal to make an arrest. Of course, since blacks were not considered citizens, they were not allowed the right to defend themselves, let alone the right to a trial if they were wrongly dragged down south. In addition, the 1850 law increased the fine for anyone caught aiding a runaway from $500 to $1,000 or $2,000, and added possible imprisonment to the penalty.[7]

One of the most famous escapees of the Underground Railroad was also a frequent guest at the Northampton Association. His name was Frederick Douglass. Although Douglass was just beginning his career during the Northampton years, he would become one of the nineteenth century's greatest black leaders. Like Truth, Douglass was born a slave. After his mistress taught him the letters of the alphabet, Douglass taught himself to read and write.[8] In 1837, he used those skills to help himself escape to freedom. Douglass saw illiteracy as a link to enslavement, so he took great pains to educate and refine himself into an articulate spokesperson for the abolition movement.

Around the time Douglass first came to Northampton, he published his autobiography, which detailed his life as a slave as well as his escape. The publicity of the book put Douglass in danger of being recaptured, because he was still considered a runaway. He fled to England, because slavery had already been abolished throughout the British Empire. Eventually, some fellow abolitionists bought his freedom, and Douglass was able to return to the United States.

Although Truth made no mention of her time with Douglass at Northampton, he made sure to mention her in a pamphlet he published about the Association:

> I met here for the first time that strange compound of wit and wisdom of wild enthusiasm and flint-like common sense, who seemed to feel it her duty to trip me up in my speeches and to ridicule my efforts to speak and act like a person of cultivation and refinement. I allude to Sojourner Truth. . . . She cared very little for elegance of speech or refinement of manner. She seemed to please herself and others best when she put her ideas in the oddest forms. She was much respected . . . for she was honest, industrious, and amiable. Her quaint speeches easily gave her an audience, and she was one of the most useful members of the Community in its day of small things.[9]

In his pamphlet, Douglass pointed out the differences between his and Truth's styles of speaking. According to him, his style was refined, while Truth's was plain. Despite their differences, however, Douglass showed how respected and valued Truth was at Northampton.

As a result of the philosophy of the Northampton Association, Truth found not only a supportive community, but began to learn about the worlds of abolition and social reform. Even after the farm closed in 1846, Truth remained in contact with other members of the community, often lecturing and traveling with them. Many of the abolitionists were Truth's friends as well as colleagues. In fact, upon the closing of the farm, one of the founders, Samuel Hill, offered to lend Truth the $300 she needed to buy her own house in the area.

The Narrative of Sojourner Truth

Although Frederick Douglass's autobiography may have put him in danger, it also became very widely read among abolitionists and was one of the most important texts of the abolition movement. On a more practical level, it was also very profitable for Douglass. The book sold forty-five hundred copies in less than six months.[10] Keeping this

Frederick Douglass, himself a former slave, was one of the most famous abolitionist speakers.

in mind, a friend from the Northampton Association named Olive Gilbert suggested that Truth publish her own autobiography. Not only would it be a means of illustrating the horrors of slavery and advancing the abolition movement, but it would also help Truth raise the money to pay back Hill for her house.

Truth began dictating her story to Gilbert in 1850, less than one year after Douglass published his autobiography. The fact that the *Narrative* was dictated, rather than written by Truth, emphasizes that there will never be a completely authoritative way of knowing exactly what Truth said or thought. Gilbert's editorial role in Truth's *Narrative* explains inaccuracies, such as why much of Truth's dialogue is written in a Southern dialect she never used in real life. Nonetheless, *The Narrative of Sojourner Truth* is a valuable source of information about her life up until 1849. Truth would later reprint the *Narrative* several times to include events that occurred after that date.

Since she already had someone to write her story, the next step for Truth was to find a publisher. Her friend William Lloyd Garrison offered to help publish the book. He put Truth in contact with a printer he knew. Garrison even wrote a promotional endorsement for Truth in the May 1850 edition of *The Liberator*.[11] Garrison no doubt saw the value of Truth's story, especially since it was unique in the fact that Truth was born a slave in the North rather than the South.

The Narrative of Sojourner Truth was printed on credit in 1850. Truth was not as well-known as Frederick Douglass, so her book was not circulated quite as much as his. This did not bother Truth. She simply began selling her own books whenever she went to abolition meetings. Eventually, she was able to save enough money to pay for the printing of the book, and more importantly, to pay for her house. At the age of fifty-seven, Truth had fulfilled one of her lifelong dreams—owning her own home. She had achieved this by speaking out about an issue in which she strongly believed—the abolition of slavery.

6

The Libyan Sibyl

As Truth became more involved with the abolitionists, she also began to get a taste for the women's rights movement. Like many abolitionists, Truth realized that women's rights activists were fighting for the same basic rights as those opposed to slavery. Many female abolitionists as well as some men crusaded for women's rights. In fact, Truth's Northampton associates, William Lloyd Garrison and Frederick Douglass, were both outspoken on the subject. Garrison included a special "Ladies Department" in his famous newspaper, *The Liberator*. He also made certain to point out in his speeches that slaves included black women.[1] As for Douglass, he was the only male to contribute to the first women's rights convention, held in Seneca Falls, New York, in 1848.

Seneca Falls

The Seneca Falls Convention was organized by some of the most influential women's rights activists in the country, including Elizabeth Cady Stanton and Lucretia Mott. Stanton was probably the best-known advocate of women's rights in the nineteenth century. She fought tirelessly for women's rights and pushed for such changes as coeducation, birth control, property rights for women, equal wages, and divorce law reform.[2] Stanton fought especially hard for women's right to vote. Without the right to vote, it was nearly impossible for women to make their voices heard in government. Stanton was chosen as the first president of the National Woman Suffrage Association in 1869. With the help of Susan B. Anthony, another famous activist, she compiled an impressive six-volume *History of Woman Suffrage* in order to document the women's suffrage movement.

Another influential woman who helped organize the Seneca Falls convention was Lucretia Mott. Mott was a Quaker schoolteacher from New York. She first became involved in the women's rights movement when she discovered that she was being paid less for doing the same work as her male colleagues. She and her husband, James, were also outspoken abolitionists. Lucretia Mott served as

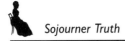
president of the American Anti-Slavery Association for several years.[3] Truth recognized the tireless work of Mott in a later edition of her *Narrative*. She called Mott "a woman whose four-score years are so replete with good words and deeds that the name falls like a benediction upon the listening ear. . . . We involuntarily bow our hearts in worship when the honored name of Lucretia Mott is pronounced."[4]

The convention Mott and Stanton organized, which was held July 19 and 20, 1848, was a gathering of women to discuss the issues most important to their cause. These issues included the social, civil, and religious conditions that affected women of the nineteenth century. On the first day, the women simply spoke among themselves. On the second day, the women decided to put their ideas down in writing, drafting the famous "Declaration of Sentiments." The document was based on the Declaration of Independence, but the women of Seneca Falls revised the original to say that all men *and* women are created equal.

Elizabeth Cady Stanton was one of the more radical leaders for women's rights. She advocated not only suffrage, but also divorce reform and birth control.

Although Stanton, Mott, and the other organizers thought the convention was a great success, only about three hundred people actually made it to Seneca Falls.[5] However, press coverage brought the event to national attention. Many male newspaper reporters and editors were upset that women were calling openly for equal rights. They accused women's rights activists of being unfeminine and called their behavior improper. One newspaper account went so far as to say that the convention was "the most shocking and unnatural incident ever recorded in the history of womanity."[6] In their attempts to belittle these women, though, such newspaper accounts gave the movement lots of free publicity. News of the Seneca Falls Convention and the Declaration of Sentiments spread well beyond the three hundred people present at the convention.

The Motts

Lucretia and James Mott were not always popular for their views. One time, a mob that did not agree with their liberal politics formed and began moving toward their house. A quick-thinking friend pretended to be a member of the mob and led the violent group in the opposite direction. The mob was so confused at not being able to find the Motts' house that it broke up and did not return.

Joining the Fight for Women's Rights

Another meeting that received a lot of negative press coverage was the first national women's rights convention, held in Worcester, Massachusetts, in October 1850. This meeting was much larger than the Seneca Falls gathering, and more speakers, including Truth, were invited to give lectures.

At first, Truth quietly listened as other women took turns speaking. Finally, it was Truth's turn. She walked up to the podium and simply asked, "Sisters, I a'n't clear what you'd be after. Ef women want any

Declaration of Rights and Sentiments

The Declaration of Rights and Sentiments adopted at the 1848 Seneca Falls Convention used similar wording to the Declaration of Independence:

When, in the course of human events, it becomes necessary for one portion of the family of man to assume among the people of the earth a position different from that which they have hitherto occupied, but one to which the laws of nature and of nature's God entitle them, a decent respect to the opinions of mankind requires that they should declare the causes that impel them to such action.

We hold these truths to be self-evident: that all men and women are created equal; that they are endowed by their Creator with certain inalienable rights; that among these are life, liberty, and the pursuit of happiness. . . .[7]

rights more'n dey's got, why don't dey jus' take 'em an' not be talkin' about it?"[8] Truth thought that it was ridiculous that women should have to fight for rights. To her, it seemed obvious that men and women should have the same rights.

At the Worcester Convention, Truth saw her old friend Garrison. When it was over, he invited Truth to come on a speaking tour with him and a British abolitionist named George Thompson. Garrison thought it would be a good opportunity for Truth to sell more of her books. He also knew that Truth's powerful public speaking was sure to be an asset to

This political cartoon mocks women's attempts to gain equal rights. Ironically, negative press like this helped bring attention to the women's rights movement nationwide.

the tour. Truth was always interested in selling more copies of her *Narrative*, but she knew she could not simply go on tour. She did not have the money to do so. Truth expressed her financial concerns to her friend. Generously, Garrison offered to pay Truth's expenses. All she had to do was meet him and Thompson in Springfield, Massachusetts.

When Truth arrived in Springfield a few months later, she learned that Garrison had fallen ill. He would not be touring with them. But Thompson still wanted Truth to be part of the tour. He asked her to continue with him, despite her friend's absence. Truth explained her financial arrangement with Garrison and said she could not afford to go without his help. Thompson assured Truth that he would be happy to pay her expenses. Truth accepted. Clearly, she was a valued member of the movement and people went to great lengths to include her.

Speaking Tours

Truth and Thompson traveled throughout the Northeast, spreading their abolitionist message. According to Truth's recollections, this was sometimes difficult. Truth remembered that the lectures were often broken up by angry mobs. Nevertheless, Truth stood her ground and continued to preach.

By early spring, Truth and Thompson had traveled extensively. They eventually wound up in Rochester, New York. There, Truth met Isaac and Amy Post, two

Bloomers

As a sign of liberation, many women involved in the women's rights movement wore "bloomers"—loose, baggy pants under a short skirt—instead of long, heavy petticoats. For Truth, however, the new fashion trend closely resembled the garments she had been forced to wear as a slave. When asked why she would not wear bloomers, Truth answered, "I had bloomers enough when I was in bondage."[9]

prominent Quaker abolitionists. The Posts' beliefs about equality and racial tolerance, as well as religion, were similar to Truth's. They often offered Truth spiritual guidance during her stays with them.[10] Amy Post was also a leading figure in the women's rights movement. She had helped organize the 1848 Seneca Falls Convention. Perhaps because of all their similar interests, she and Truth became close friends and would correspond for most of Truth's life.

The Akron Convention Speech

Truth stayed with the Posts for several months. By winter's end, though, she once again felt a call to travel. This time she was being called west. Truth heard that the second women's rights convention was to be held in Akron, Ohio, in May 1851. A famous antislavery newspaper called the *Anti-Slavery*

Bugle invited "all the friends of Reform, in whatever department engaged" to attend.[11] Truth knew she had to be there.

It was at this convention that Truth made her famous Akron speech, which combined the two great struggles of her life—abolition and women's rights. As she proudly walked up to the podium, Truth made her presence known as a black person and as a woman. She made it clear that the women's rights movement should not exclude blacks, nor should the abolitionists exclude women. In other words, Sojourner Truth believed that neither racism nor sexism should be tolerated. Truth's speech later became immortalized when Frances Gage published a version of it in the April 23, 1863, issue of the New York *Independent* newspaper. It was reprinted again in the 1870s in Truth's updated *Narrative*.

After Akron, Truth continued lecturing in the Midwest. She borrowed a horse and buggy from friends and spent the next two years traveling, lecturing, and selling her book.[12]

Continuing Her Lecture Tour

It was not long after the Akron Convention that Truth once again brought attention to herself and her causes. In 1852, in Salem, Ohio, Truth was listening to Frederick Douglass speak at an anniversary meeting of an antislavery society. Douglass was growing frustrated with the slow progress of the abolition movement. Going against his Garrisonian philosophy of peaceful resolution, Douglass suggested that violence might be the only way to end black oppression. At this, Truth immediately jumped up from the audience and asked her colleague, "Frederick, *is God dead?*"[13] Even at the worst of times, Truth did not lose faith in her beliefs, nor would she accept violence as a possible solution.

During another lecture in her Midwest tour, Truth was heckled by a man in the audience. He accused her of not supporting the Constitution of the United States. With a sparkle in her eye, Truth told a story to set the man straight. It revolved around a kind of beetle, called a weevil, that had ruined the wheat crop in Ohio that year.

"Children," she said,

> I talk to God and God talks to me. I go out and talk to God in the fields and the woods. This morning I was walking out, and I got over the fence. I saw the wheat holding up its head, looking very big. I go up and take hold of it. You believe it, there was *no* wheat there? I say "God, what *is* the matter with *this* wheat?" And he says to me, "Sojourner, there is a little weevil in it."
>
> Now I hear talking about this Constitution and the rights of man. I come up and I take hold of this Constitution. It looks *mighty big*, and I feel for *my* rights, but there ain't any there. Then I say "God, what *ails* this Constitution?" He says to me, "Sojourner, there is a little weevil in it."[14]

Through humor, Truth pointed out a fault in the Constitution—namely that it did not truly provide for the rights of *all* people.

Harriet Beecher Stowe

By 1853, Truth was ready to head east. On her way back to her house in Northampton, Truth decided to stop by the home of a very influential author of the time—Harriet Beecher Stowe. Stowe was the author of *Uncle Tom's Cabin, or Life Among the Lowly*, written in 1852. It is the story of a slave named Tom and the hardships he endures under his horribly cruel master, Simon Legree. Stowe decided to write the novel in response to the harsh Fugitive Slave Law of 1850. The novel was extremely influential in opening people's eyes to the true horrors of slavery. It was also a huge commercial success. In just the first week of publication, the book sold ten thousand copies![15]

As the story goes, Truth appeared one day at Stowe's home in Andover, Massachusetts. Stowe had a house full of company that day but was very taken with Truth. Stowe would later write, "I do not recollect ever to have been conversant with any one who had more of that silent and subtle power which we call personal presence than this woman." In fact, Stowe was so impressed that she invited Truth to come inside and join her guests. The group talked for hours about Truth's life, adventures, and most of

Harriet Beecher Stowe's novel Uncle Tom's Cabin *was as influential as it was successful.*

all, her famous opinions. Truth even sang some of her hymns for them. As Stowe said, "no princess could have received a drawing-room with more composed dignity than Sojourner her audience."[16]

Before Truth left, she asked Stowe to sign her *Book of Life*. The *Book of Life* was Truth's collection of newspaper clippings and autographs of famous people she met on her journeys. It was later reprinted in a new edition of the *Narrative*.

Stowe eventually did much more for Truth than simply sign her book. Ten years later, Stowe wrote an article recounting her meeting with Truth. The essay, called "The Libyan Sibyl," appeared in the April 1863 issue of the famous magazine *Atlantic Monthly*. In addition to the story of their meeting, Stowe's article also contained biographical information on Truth. Most importantly, it increased Truth's fame and helped her cement the reputation she had already begun building for herself.

Selling the Shadow

As Truth's fame grew, she decided to add to her publicity through another means—photographs. During the late 1850s and 1860s, it was very popular to buy and sell small postcards with people's pictures on them. They were called cartes de visites. Truth had several cartes de visites of herself made up with the phrase "I sell the shadow to support the substance" printed on the bottom. The slogan

Sojourner Truth sold these portraits of herself to raise money while she traveled on lecture tours.

explained why Truth was selling the cards in the first place—to support herself during her crusade against slavery. She sold them at meetings along with her book.

No sooner had Truth returned to Northampton than she traveled to New York City for another speaking engagement. The crowd that gathered there on September 8, 1853, was particularly hostile. Some had paid a twenty-five-cent admission just to have the chance to heckle the women speakers.[17] When Truth appeared, they became even more rowdy. To these closed-minded men, she represented "the two most hated elements of humanity. She was black and she was a woman."[18]

Truth never publicly showed any discouragement. She kept on speaking out at all costs. At one meeting, a man questioned the validity of her work. He asked: "Old woman, do you think that your talk about slavery does any good? Do you suppose people care what you say? Why, I don't care any more for your talk than I do for the bite of a flea." Undaunted, Truth quickly replied, "Perhaps not, but, the Lord willing, I'll keep you scratching."[19]

7

SOJOURNER TRUTH GOES TO WASHINGTON

By the late 1850s, tension was brewing between the North and the South. The Southern states were growing increasingly fearful that the Northern states were trying to end slavery, and in so doing, take over most of the political power in the nation. The North, on the other hand, feared that the Southern states were trying to spread slavery to new western territories in order to win more political power for themselves. While Truth was obviously interested in these debates, she never actively engaged in the politics concerning them. In fact, around 1857 it looked as if Truth were semi-retired.

During her travels, Truth had visited Battle Creek, Michigan, a city that was known for its progressive attitudes and racial tolerance. In 1857, Truth decided to sell her house in Northampton and move to Michigan. At first, she lived in Harmonia, a community six miles from Battle Creek. Truth's daughters, Diana and Elizabeth, and their two sons, Samuel Banks and James Caldwell, went with her to Harmonia. Of all her grandchildren, Truth was particularly close to Sammy. He became her traveling companion and accompanied her on almost all her adventures and speaking tours.

By 1860, Truth sold the house in Harmonia to her daughter Sophia in order to move to Battle Creek. In Battle Creek, Truth's daughters hoped their mother would relax a bit. Perhaps for a short time she did. However, with the country becoming more divided over issues such as slavery and states' rights, it was inevitable that Truth would not be able to sit still for long.

Dred Scott, John Brown, and the Fight Over Slavery

The same year Truth moved to Michigan, the United States Supreme Court ruled on the infamous *Dred Scott* case. Dred Scott was a Missouri slave who had moved with his master to the free state of Illinois and the free territory of Minnesota. Because he had lived on free soil, Scott decided to sue his master for his freedom. The case went all the way to the Supreme Court. In the end, the Supreme Court decided that Scott did not have the right to sue, since he was not a United States citizen. According to the Court, no black person could be a citizen. The ruling was a blow to the abolition movement. It meant that black Americans, even those who were free like Truth, were ineligible for United States citizenship and its privileges.

Tensions over slavery sometimes led to violence. Throughout much of the nineteenth century, there were many slave uprisings in which groups of slaves violently rebelled against their white masters in hopes of winning their freedom. One of the worst incidents, however, was led not by a slave but by a militant white abolitionist named John Brown.

Although John Brown had long been outspoken and well-known for his stance on slavery, he became most famous for leading a violent raid in Virginia in 1859. Brown planned to free slaves through force, then train them as soldiers to attack slaveholders and free other slaves. In October 1859, he organized an attack on a military arsenal at Harpers Ferry, Virginia (now West Virginia). He planned to use the weapons he would steal to free more slaves. Brown's plans failed, however, when United States Marines put down the rebellion. Brown was tried, found guilty of treason, and on December 2, 1859, he was hanged. Many abolitionists in the North considered

Militant abolitionist John Brown led a failed raid on Harpers Ferry in 1859. Hated by the South, Brown was considered a martyr by many abolitionists after he was executed.

Brown a hero for his attack against slavery. Southerners, on the other hand, feared further attacks and took steps to increase their military preparations in case of another slave revolt—or a war.

The Road to Civil War

More fuel was added to the fire in 1860, with the upcoming presidential election. Truth particularly liked one of the candidates because of his stance against the spread of slavery. His name was Abraham Lincoln.

As a Republican political leader, Lincoln did not aggressively work to outlaw slavery, but he did fight to confine it to states where it already existed. In 1854, Lincoln had spoken out against Senator Stephen Douglas's proposal—the famous Kansas-Nebraska bill. The bill gave citizens who lived in these newly created territories the right to vote whether they wanted to be admitted to the Union as a free state or a slave state. Despite criticism from politicians such as Lincoln, the bill passed in May 1854, but it caused many more problems than it solved.

Proslavery forces from Missouri crossed the border into the Kansas territory in order to try to swing the vote. Most of the citizens of Kansas, however, wanted to be admitted as a free state. When the supporters of slavery won the vote, the antislavery residents refused to acknowledge it or the new state government. The incident led to violence with attacks and counterattacks from both sides.

While abolitionists were somewhat mixed about their opinions of Lincoln, Southerners were dead set in theirs. They disliked his politics so much that they promised to secede—leave the Union—if he were elected president. In 1860, Lincoln won the election without a single Southern vote. To a large degree, Lincoln, the Republican candidate, won the election because the Democratic party split, nominating two candidates: Stephen Douglas for the Northern Democrats and John Breckinridge for the Southern Democrats. True to their word, seven states of the Deep South seceded before Lincoln took office in March 1861 and formed the Confederate States of America. The country seemed destined for civil war.

Civil War

As of April 12, 1861, there was no longer any doubt. Confederate troops attacked Fort Sumter, in Charleston, South Carolina, and the Civil War officially began. Although Truth still did not advocate violence, she gave her full support to the Union once war was declared.

In 1862, an old abolitionist friend named Josephine Griffing came to visit Truth in Michigan. Griffing invited Truth to join a new lecture tour. Truth immediately agreed and once again began

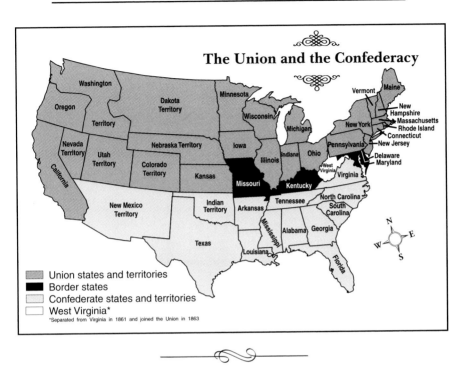

The Union and the Confederacy

Union states and territories
Border states
Confederate states and territories
West Virginia*

*Separated from Virginia in 1861 and joined the Union in 1863

During the Civil War, the states were divided in loyalty between the Union and the Confederacy.

traveling and speaking out against slavery just as passionately as ever. On one occasion, Griffing remembered Truth angrily telling a hostile crowd, "It seems that it takes *my* black face to bring out *your* black hearts; so it's well I came."[1] As usual, Truth wanted to make it clear that slavery and those who supported it were morally wrong.

Finally, on January 1, 1863, it looked as if the abolition movement had made some real progress. President Lincoln signed the Emancipation Proclamation, freeing slaves in the Confederate states. It

President Lincoln signed the Emancipation Proclamation on January 1, 1863. It freed slaves in areas still under Confederate control. However, all slaves were not actually freed until 1865, when the Thirteenth Amendment was ratified.

said: "All persons held as slaves within any State or designated part of a State, the people whereof shall . . . be in rebellion against the United States, shall be then, thenceforward, and forever free."[2]

This was a major step for one of Truth's causes. However, the fight was far from over, especially since the country was in the middle of a war. Furthermore, the declaration by no means guaranteed black Americans equal rights. In fact, black men had not even been allowed to join the Union Army, despite the fact that many wanted to take an active part in the fight for their freedom. Along with other black leaders, most notably Frederick Douglass, Truth campaigned for the Union Army to accept black troops. By 1863, President Lincoln yielded to the abolitionist demand, and by April, the first black regiment, the Massachusetts 54th, was formed. Soon black men from across the Union were volunteering to serve. Among those brave men were Truth's grandson James Caldwell and two of Frederick Douglass's sons.

As her grandson fought on the front lines, Truth fought from behind them. She went door to door, collecting food for local troops. In one famous anecdote, a man refused to donate to Truth's food drive. She asked him his name and he replied, "I am the only son of my mother." Truth quickly retorted, "I am glad there are no more," and continued to the next house.[3]

Abolitionists, including Truth and Douglass, fought to allow black soldiers to fight for the Union. As a result, all-black units such as this one were formed.

Truth also composed songs to boost the troops' morale. Her most famous was "The Valiant Soldiers," sung to the tune of the "Battle Hymn of the Republic." In the last verse, Truth told the story of Lincoln's allowing black soldiers to fight:

> *Father Abraham has spoken, and the message*
> *   has been sent;*
> *The prison doors have opened, and out the*
> *   prisoners went*
> *To join the sable army of African descent,*
> *As we go marching on—*[4]

Washington, D.C., 1864

Truth was thrilled with the progress the abolitionists were making. She decided that she would go down to Washington, D.C., and tell the president himself how pleased she was with his work. Truth made her way to Washington, D.C., with her grandson Sammy, visiting friends and lecturing along the way. Truth never doubted that Lincoln would meet with her. "I shall surely go," she said. "I never determined to do anything and failed."[5]

As usual, Truth succeeded in doing what she put her mind to. On October 29, 1864, she met President Abraham Lincoln. Truth conveyed the story in a letter to a friend, which was then published in a later volume of her *Narrative*. Truth told Lincoln he was "the best president who has ever taken the seat."[6] Lincoln was flattered, but said there were others, particularly George Washington, who were much better presidents than he was. Before leaving, Truth made certain to ask the president to sign her *Book of Life*. He wrote: "For Aunty Sojourner Truth, Oct. 29, 1864. A. Lincoln." Truth was very proud to have his autograph. As she left, she thought to herself, "I felt that I was in the presence of a friend, and I now thank God from the bottom of my heart that I always have advocated his cause."[7]

At the time Truth was in Washington, D.C., the city was not a very pleasant place to live, particularly

Sojourner Truth met with President Abraham Lincoln in 1864.

for the poor and uneducated. After emancipation, former slaves from Maryland and Virginia fled to the nation's capital in hopes of starting a new life. Unfortunately, although they were free, it was clear that black Americans' problems were not miraculously solved with their emancipation. With no money and little education or skills, it was difficult to find jobs or support themselves. Many of these former slaves were forced to live in overcrowded and unhealthy areas of the city.

The Freedmen's Bureau

In order to help, abolitionists created relief organizations to help black Americans make the transition from slavery to freedom. Toward the end of the war, the federal government began funding similar relief efforts by creating the Bureau of Refugees, Freedmen, and Abandoned Lands.[8] Known as the Freedmen's Bureau, the agency was set up to protect the rights of newly freed slaves, to temporarily provide them with food and shelter, to educate them, and to teach them a trade so they could find work.

Truth worked in both the abolitionists' and the federally funded organizations from 1864 to 1868. Her assignment for the Freedmen's Bureau was as a counselor at Freedmen's Village, located at Arlington Heights, Virginia—the former estate of Confederate General Robert E. Lee. At the village, Truth taught women domestic tasks such as cooking and sewing.

Through the efforts of the Freedmen's Bureau, ex-slaves learned everyday skills such as sewing.

She was a stickler when it came to cleaning. She always insisted that the residents at the village be neat and clean. Truth could often be heard chiding, "Be clean! be clean! for cleanliness is godliness."[9]

While still working for the Freedmen's Bureau, Truth heard the wonderful news that the war was over. On April 9, 1865, Confederate General Robert E. Lee was surrounded at Appomattox Court House, Virginia. He surrendered to Union General Ulysses S. Grant, which marked the approaching end of the Civil War.

The good tidings did not last long, however. Five days later, on April 14, President Lincoln was shot by an actor and Confederate sympathizer named John Wilkes Booth while watching a play at Ford's Theatre in Washington, D.C. Lincoln died the next day. After Lincoln's death, Vice President Andrew Johnson succeeded him.

Reconstruction

Truth encouraged the freedmen not to lose hope. It was hard to keep morale up, though, especially since blacks still had no say in lawmaking processes. All

United States senators celebrate the passage of the Thirteenth Amendment, which banned slavery.

that changed during Reconstruction, the period after the Civil War during which the Southern states were brought back into the Union. In 1865, the Thirteenth Amendment to the Constitution officially abolished slavery throughout the United States. It was not until 1870, after the Fifteenth Amendment to the United States Constitution was ratified, that the status of the freedmen finally changed. The amendment declared: "The right of citizens of the United States to vote shall not be denied or abridged by the United States or by any State on account of race, color, or previous condition of servitude." In theory, black citizens now had the same rights as white citizens, which meant they could vote and run for public office.

The news was only half good, though. While it granted black men the right to vote, women of all colors were still excluded. Many women's rights activists who had worked for abolition felt betrayed. On hearing the news that only men had won the right to vote, Truth said:

> There is a great stir about colored men getting their rights, but not a word about the colored women; and if colored men get their rights, and not colored women theirs, you see the colored men will be masters over the women, and it will be just as bad as it was before.[10]

Unfortunately, Truth and many of her fellow women's rights activists would not live to see the day that women's suffrage was won. The Nineteenth

Amendment granting women the right to vote would not be ratified until 1920.

As a black woman, Truth had to deal with problems of her own in Washington, D.C. In order to get from place to place in the city, Truth often took streetcars. Although there was a law banning segregation—the practice of separating people by race—on the cars, some white passengers tried to give Truth a hard time for wanting to ride. Truth was very aware that she had the same right as everyone else in the city to ride the cars and would not let anyone tell her differently.

On one occasion, Truth signaled for several cars to stop, but none did. At the top of her voice, she yelled, "I want to ride! *I want to ride!! I WANT TO RIDE!!!*"[11] Everyone was so surprised to see an elderly black woman screaming on the street corner, that not only did the streetcar stop, but all the traffic and passers-by as well. Truth quickly stepped on, much to

A famous illustration of the first black vote after the Civil War.

the dismay of the conductor, who had tried to pass her. Several of the passengers laughed at the way Truth had triumphed over the conductor.

Another time, Truth was traveling with her friend Laura Haviland, a wealthy white woman. As the streetcar stopped in front of the two women, Truth stepped forward to get on first. The conductor was very angry and pushed Truth out of the way, telling her to let the lady on first. Truth replied, "I am a lady too," and again tried get on. The conductor did not stop there. He grabbed Truth by the shoulder and violently tried to shove her out the

Women's Suffrage

Women's rights activists were particularly disappointed in the fact that women were excluded from the guaranteed rights of the Fourteenth and Fifteenth amendments. They had been working for years to prevent just such an outcome. In an 1866 letter to Truth, famous suffrage leader Susan B. Anthony wrote:

Do you know that there are three men . . . who have dared to propose to amend the United States Constitution by inserting the word "male," thus shutting all women out by constitution from voting. . . . It is a most atrocious proposition, and I know Sojourner Truth will say, No, to it. God bless you, and help you to do the good work before you.[12]

door. Haviland told him to let her friend go at once, but he would not listen. He asked the white woman if Truth belonged to her. Angrily, she replied, "No, . . . She belongs to humanity." The conductor once again shoved Truth against the door, this time so hard that he dislocated her shoulder.[13] The two women got off the car, but their fight certainly was not over. They wrote down the number of the car and reported the offense the next day. Truth had the conductor arrested on charges of assault and battery. Eventually, he lost his job because of the way he had treated Truth and her friend. Despite the fact that she was in her late sixties, Truth was still fighting for her rights and her beliefs with the same energy she had as a young woman.

$\boxed{8}$

ONE LAST MISSION

Despite the efforts of the Freedmen's Bureau, conditions for African Americans were not significantly improving. Washington, D.C., alone had more than twenty thousand freedmen, and no matter how well trained they became, there simply were not enough jobs to go around.[1] Advocates of the bureau were always fighting for more federal funding, but such Reconstruction programs were very controversial. For every person who argued that the Freedmen's Bureau needed more money, there was always someone else to insist it was not the government's job to help black Americans.

Watching poor, often homeless, free blacks living in the street without food or money, reminded

This political cartoon illustrates the debate between those who believed the Freedmen's Bureau needed more money and those who thought freed blacks had already received more than they should have. The Freedmen's Bureau is depicted as a soldier, standing between whites and newly freed slaves to prevent violence.

Truth of the reason she had left New York City so many years before. She could not bear Washington any longer and felt it was time to move on. But before leaving, Truth decided that, if no one would find a solution to the problems that plagued the freed slaves, she would have to try to find one herself.

Working to Help the Freedmen

As Truth's position at the Freedmen's Village ended and she prepared to leave the city, she tried to think of possible ways to help improve living conditions. At first, Truth found jobs and homes up north for some of the freedmen she had come to know. In her *Narrative*, Truth claimed she made three trips from Rochester, New York, to a town two hundred miles south of Richmond, Virginia, in order to connect young men with positions she had found.[2] After a short while, though, Truth was no longer certain that this was the best plan of action. Since she could only find jobs for strong, young men, the women, children, and elderly were still left in poverty to fend for themselves.

Truth continued to watch conditions worsen despite her efforts. Soon, though, she thought of a new and better way to help. Truth believed that the United States government should set aside uninhabited land in the West to give the newly freed blacks, in the same way that reservations had been set aside for American Indians. Truth felt that her plan to obtain land grants would improve the miserable conditions in which free blacks lived. Truth also believed that allotting uninhabited land was the least the government could do for black Americans, considering all they had been through. "Our nerves and sinews, our tears and blood, have been sacrificed on the altar of this nation's avarice [greed]. Our unpaid labor has been a stepping-stone to its financial success. Some of its dividends must surely be ours," proclaimed Truth.[3] If African Americans were given land to cultivate on their own, they would surely be more independent and resourceful than they would if left homeless and uneducated in the squalor of big cities.

Truth's task was doubly hard. Not only did she have to convince freed blacks to relocate, but she had to convince the government to allot the land as well. Just as she had done in her abolitionist days, Truth tackled the problem by speaking out publicly. Much of her argument was based on an appeal to rich white men's pockets. Truth contended that too many black men lived off the government, thereby costing a lot in taxes. If freedmen were given their own land, they would have a greater incentive to support themselves, making them more productive members of society.[4]

A Boston newspaper reported on an 1871 speech Truth gave on the eighth anniversary of the

Emancipation Proclamation, where she argued that the United States should give freed slaves land and "move them on it." "[G]et de ole pepul out," she said, "and build dem homes in de West where dey can feed themselves, and dey would soon be abel to be a pepul among you. Dat is my commission."[5]

Truth was also very concerned with educating African Americans in their potential new homes. She understood firsthand the difficulties of not being able to read and write. Therefore, she advocated education as a means of liberation.

As usual, Truth did not stop with lecturing. She believed the most direct way to get the government to listen to her was to speak to the government itself. So, she drafted a petition to Congress:

> To the Senate and House of Representatives, in Congress assembled:—
>
> *Whereas,* From the faithful and earnest representations of Sojourner Truth (who has personally investigated the matter), we believe that the freed colored people in and about Washington, dependent upon government for support, would be greatly benefited and might become useful citizens by being placed in a position to support themselves: We, the undersigned, therefore earnestly request your honorable body to set apart for them a portion of the public land in the West, and erect buildings thereon for the aged and infirm, and otherwise legislate so as to secure the desired results.[6]

Truth felt that the land grant project would be the culmination of her life work. Even though she was over seventy years old, she continued touring and speaking in order to win support for her proposal and signatures for her petition. She hoped to get enough signatures to "send tons of paper down to Washington."[7] Before she left to tour, Truth's friend Frances Titus offered to update her *Narrative*. The new version was published in 1875. It included news clippings, letters, and autographs from her *Book of Life*. As with the original version, Truth brought copies of her updated *Narrative* to sell at the meetings at which she spoke.

Although many people were willing to sign her petition, Truth was unable to find a senator willing to present it in Congress. Without any powerful political allies, she could not push her land grant mission any further.

In early 1875, Truth received some more bad news that put an end to her land grant project for the time. Her beloved grandson and companion, Sammy, was very ill. Truth rushed back to her home in Battle Creek to be with him. While she made it back in time to see him, he did not live much longer. He died in February 1875 at the age of twenty-four.

The time immediately following Sammy's death was very hard for Truth. Aside from his death, the Freedmen's Bureau had been cut off from federal funding. Truth had yet to find someone to present her petition to Congress, and it looked like she never would. As the years passed, it seemed that the government was becoming less concerned with the people it had helped to free.

Westward Migration

Then, in 1879, something astonishing happened. Tens of thousands of poor black freedmen began fleeing Southern states such as Mississippi and Louisiana and relocating to Kansas of their own accord.[8] Kansas was still a relatively unpopulated state, so it offered freedmen a chance to start a new life.

Since the government was doing very little to protect or help them, African Americans were afraid that life in the South would revert to the way it had been before the war. While African Americans were legally granted the same rights as whites, many white Southerners refused to accept the law. Segregation laws, known as Jim Crow laws, were passed by whites to separate the races. Some radically racist groups, such as the Ku Klux Klan, resorted to violence and even murder to keep blacks from achieving equal rights. Fearful that their hard won independence was in danger, some black families thought it better to relocate.

Although it was not exactly the plan she had envisioned, Truth was thrilled that freedmen were taking their future into their own hands. Relief organizations similar to those set up in Washington, D.C., after the war were established to help the migrants get settled. For a time, Truth volunteered

This political cartoon by Thomas Nast shows how white supremacist groups worked together after the Civil War to keep African Americans in a state of fear and poverty.

at the newly formed Kansas Freedmen's Relief Association along with her old friends Frances Titus and Laura Haviland.

By 1879, the migration had tapered off, and Truth, now in her eighties, was exhausted. She moved back to Battle Creek in January 1880. There, she lived with her daughters and their children.

By 1883, Sojourner Truth had fallen seriously ill. She died on November 26. Her funeral was one of the biggest Battle Creek had ever seen. Many of her famous colleagues, including Frederick Douglass, William Lloyd Garrison, and Elizabeth Cady Stanton, eulogized her.[9] Even at the end, Truth's legend was larger than life.

9

KEEP THEM SCRATCHING

It is difficult to sum up Sojourner Truth's legacy with just one word. She was a supporter of many types of social reform in nineteenth-century America. Determined and aggressive, Truth let neither her race nor her gender keep her from pursuing her goals. As an abolitionist, she worked tirelessly alongside some of the most famous antislavery voices of the day. For her work as a women's rights activist, Truth was remembered by Elizabeth Cady Stanton as "the most wonderful woman the colored race has ever produced."[1]

But perhaps Truth did not want to be remembered as just a woman *or* as just a black person. She took pride in being a *black woman* and fought hard to remind people of that very fact. Truth forced mostly male abolitionists to recognize that female slaves needed freedom as much as male slaves did, while pointing out to predominantly white women's rights activists that women of color should be included in their cause as well.

Despite the nation's flaws, Truth believed in the United States, and more importantly, she believed in the potential to change its flaws. She overcame slavery, poverty, and other hardships to become a strong presence in the fight for equality. In times of grief or failure—such as the departure of her son from New York or the government's refusal to help her land grant project—Truth still continued her struggle.

Truth's story has inspired generations of activists to do the same. African Americans have struggled for full equality from Truth's time, through the civil rights movement of the 1950s and 1960s, and even to the present day. Likewise, although women were granted the right to vote in 1920, they have fought throughout the twentieth century to win many of the same rights as men. In the end, it is in this shared belief in the equality of all people that the legacy of Sojourner Truth lives on. Her strong belief in God, her family, herself, and the causes for which she continually fought have earned her a much deserved place in the history of American social reform.

CHRONOLOGY

c. 1797 — Born in Hurley, New York.

1808 — Sold to the Nealys.

1809 — Sold to the Schrivers.

1810 — Sold to the Dumonts.

1814 — Married to Thomas, another of Dumont's slaves.

1815 — Gives birth to five children: Diana, Peter, Elizabeth,
-1826 Sophia, and Thomas.

1826 — Leaves Dumont and gains freedom.

1828 — Son Peter is returned after Truth wins a lawsuit; Moves to New York City.

1832 — Meets Pierson and Matthias; Joins the Kingdom of Matthias.

1839 — Peter leaves New York.

1843 — Leaves New York City and moves to Northampton, Massachusetts; Takes the name Sojourner Truth.

1850 — Publishes *The Narrative of Sojourner Truth*; Speaks at the first women's rights convention in Worcester, Massachusetts.

1851 — Gives famous speech at second women's rights convention in Akron, Ohio.

1853 — Meets Harriet Beecher Stowe in Andover, Massachusetts.

1857 — Moves to Battle Creek, Michigan, with daughters and grandsons.

1863 — Frances Gage's version of Truth's Akron speech is published; Stowe publishes "The Libyan Sibyl" in the *Atlantic Monthly*.

1864 — Works in Washington, D.C., with freedmen.
-1868

1875 — New edition of *Narrative* published with *Book of Life*.

1883 — Dies in Battle Creek, Michigan.

Chapter Notes

Chapter 1. "Ain't I a Woman?"

1. Olive Gilbert, *The Narrative of Sojourner Truth*, ed. Henry Louis Gates (New York: Oxford University Press, 1991), pp. 131–135.

2. Andrea Atkin, "Sojourner Truth," *The Historical Encyclopedia of World Slavery*, ed. Junius P. Rodriguez (Santa Barbara, Calif.: ABC-CLIO, 1997), vol. 2, pp. 651–652.

3. Ibid.

4. Wendy Hamand Venet, *Neither Ballots Nor Bullets: Women Abolitionists and the Civil War* (Charlottesville: University Press of Virginia, 1991), p. 12.

5. Gilbert, pp. 131–132.

6. Ibid., p. 132.

7. Elizabeth Cady Stanton et al., eds., *History of Woman Suffrage* (New York: Fowler and Wells, 1881–1922), vol. 1, pp. 101–103.

8. Gilbert, p. 134.

Chapter 2. A Slave Named Isabella

1. Nell Irvin Painter, *Sojourner Truth: A Life, a Symbol* (New York: W. W. Norton and Co., 1996), p. 12.

2. Olive Gilbert, *The Narrative of Sojourner Truth*, ed. Henry Louis Gates (New York: Oxford University Press, 1991), p. 17.

3. Ibid.

4. Ibid., p. 16.

5. Ibid., p. 17.

6. Ibid., pp. 108–109.

7. Ibid., p. 26.

8. Ibid.

9. Ibid., p. 27.

10. Ibid., p. 28.

11. Ibid., pp. 24–25.

12. Patricia McKissack and Frederick McKissack, *Sojourner Truth: Ain't I a Woman?* (New York: Scholastic, Inc., 1992), p. 124.

13. Painter, p. 14.

14. Gilbert, p. 33.

15. Painter, p. 15.

16. Gilbert, pp. 31–32.

Chapter 3. Freedom

1. Olive Gilbert, *The Narrative of Sojourner Truth*, ed. Henry Louis Gates (New York: Oxford University Press, 1991), pp. 35–36.

2. Ibid., p. 38.

3. John Callow, "New York," *The Historical Encyclopedia of Slavery*, ed. Junius Rodriguez (Santa Barbara, Calif.: ABC-CLIO, 1997), vol. 2, p. 467.

4. Nell Irvin Painter, *Sojourner Truth: A Life, a Symbol* (New York: W. W. Norton and Co., 1996), p. 25.

5. Gilbert, p. 43.

6. Ibid., p. 124.

7. Ibid., p. 44.

8. Ibid., p. 45.

9. Ibid.

10. Ibid., pp. 69–72.

Chapter 4. Isabella in the City

1. Nell Irvin Painter, *Sojourner Truth: A Life, a Symbol* (New York: W. W. Norton and Co., 1996), p. 38.

2. Olive Gilbert, *The Narrative of Sojourner Truth*, ed. Henry Louis Gates (New York: Oxford University Press, 1991), p. 71.

3. Ibid., p. 81.

4. Jacqueline Bernard, *Journey Toward Freedom: The Story of Sojourner Truth* (New York: W. W. Norton & Co., 1967), pp. 102–103.

5. Gilbert, p. 93.

6. Painter, p. 55.

7. Paul E. Johnson and Sean Wilentz, *The Kingdom of Matthias* (New York: Oxford University Press, 1994), p. 97.

8. Ibid.

9. Bernard, p. 106.

10. Gilbert, p. 77.

11. Ibid., pp. 77–79.

12. Ibid., p. 103.

13. Ibid., p. 98.

14. Ibid., p. 100.

Chapter 5. Abolition

1. Olive Gilbert, *The Narrative of Sojourner Truth*, ed. Henry Louis Gates (New York: Oxford University Press, 1991), p. 114.

2. Ibid., p. 116.

3. Ibid., p. 117.

4. Erlene Stetson and Linda David, *Glorying in Tribulation: The Lifework of Sojourner Truth* (East Lansing: Michigan State University Press, 1994), p. 100.

5. Alive Eaton McBee, *From Utopia to Florence: The Story of a Transcendentalist Community in Northampton, Mass., 1830–1850* (Philadelphia: Porcupine Press, 1975), p. 22.

6. Gilbert, p. 120.

7. Jane H. Pease and William H. Pease, *The Fugitive Slave Law and Anthony Burns: A Problem in Law Enforcement* (Philadelphia: Lippincott, 1975), pp. 11–12.

8. Frederick Douglass, *Narrative of the Life of Frederick Douglass, an American Slave*, ed. Houston A. Baker, Jr. (New York: Viking Penguin, 1986), pp. 77–87.

9. Quoted in McBee, pp. i–ii.

10. William L. Andrews, *To Tell a Free Story: The First Century of Afro-American Autobiography, 1760–1865* (Urbana: University of Illinois Press, 1986), pp. 97, 138.

11. Nell Irvin Painter, *Sojourner Truth: A Life, a Symbol* (New York: W. W. Norton and Co., 1996), p. 111.

Chapter 6. The Libyan Sibyl

1. Wendy Hamand Venet, *Neither Ballots Nor Bullets: Women Abolitionists and the Civil War* (Charlottesville: University Press of Virginia, 1991), p. 3.

2. Elisabeth Griffith, *In Her Own Right: The Life of Elizabeth Cady Stanton* (New York: Oxford University Press, 1984), p. xiv.

3. Constance Burnett, *Five for Freedom: Lucretia Mott, Elizabeth Cady Stanton, Lucy Stone, Susan B. Anthony, Carrie Chapman Catt* (New York: Greenwood Press, 1968), p. 31.

4. Olive Gilbert, *The Narrative of Sojourner Truth*, ed. Henry Louis Gates (New York: Oxford University Press, 1991), p. 318.

5. Miriam Gurko, *The Ladies of Seneca Falls: The Birth of the Woman's Rights Movement* (New York: Schocken Books, 1976), pp. 102–103.

6. Ibid.

7. Jerome B. Agel, ed., "Woman is Man's Equal: Women's Rights, 1848," *Words That Make America Great* (New York: Random House, 1997), p. 112.

8. Gurko, p. 165.

9. Gilbert, p. 165.

10. Nell Irvin Painter, *Sojourner Truth: A Life, a Symbol* (New York: W. W. Norton and Co., 1996), p. 143.

11. Ibid., p. 120.

12. Jacqueline Bernard, *Journey Toward Freedom: The Story of Sojourner Truth* (New York: W. W. Norton & Co., 1967), p. 171.

13. Gilbert, p. 168.

14. Quoted in Erlene Stetson and Linda David, *Glorying in Tribulation: The Lifework of Sojourner Truth* (East Lansing: Michigan State University Press, 1994), p. 132.

15. Joan D. Hedrick, *Harriet Beecher Stowe: A Life* (New York: Oxford University Press, 1994), p. 223.

16. Gilbert, pp. 151–153.

17. Stetson and David, p. 136.

18. Elizabeth Cady Stanton et al., eds., *History of Woman Suffrage* (New York: Fowler and Wells, 1881–1922), vol. 1, p. 567.

19. Gilbert, p. 312.

Chapter 7. Sojourner Truth Goes to Washington

1. Nell Irvin Painter, *Sojourner Truth: A Life, a Symbol* (New York: W. W. Norton and Co., 1996), p. 181.

2. John Hope Franklin, *The Emancipation Proclamation* (New York: Anchor Books, 1965), p. 91.

3. Painter, p. 182.

4. Olive Gilbert, *The Narrative of Sojourner Truth*, ed. Henry Louis Gates (New York: Oxford University Press, 1991), p. 126.

5. Ibid., p. 175.

6. Ibid., p. 178.

7. Ibid., p. 179.

8. Painter, p. 213.

9. Gilbert, p. 182.

10. Quoted in Patricia McKissack and Fredrick McKissack, *Sojourner Truth: Ain't I a Woman?* (New York: Scholastic Books, Inc., 1992), p. 154.

11. Gilbert, p. 184.

12. Ibid., p. 28.

13. Ibid., p. 282.

Chapter 8. One Last Mission

1. Jacqueline Bernard, *Journey Toward Freedom: The Story of Sojourner Truth* (New York: W. W. Norton & Co., 1967), p. 222.

2. Olive Gilbert, *The Narrative of Sojourner Truth*, ed. Henry Louis Gates (New York: Oxford University Press, 1991), p. 191.

3. Ibid., p. 197.

4. Ibid., pp. 215–216.

5. Ibid., pp. 215–217.

6. Ibid., p. 199.

7. Ibid., p. 220.

8. Nell Irvin Painter, *Sojourner Truth: A Life, a Symbol* (New York: W. W. Norton and Co., 1996), p. 243.

9. Ibid., pp. 254–255.

Chapter 9. Keep Them Scratching

1. Elizabeth Cady Stanton et al., eds., *History of Woman Suffrage* (New York: Fowler and Wells, 1881–1922) vol. 3, pp. 531–532.

GLOSSARY

abolitionist—A person who worked to do away with slavery.

arsenal—A place where weapons are made and stored.

communal—As a group; in common.

Confederate States of America—The eleven states that withdrew from the United Sates in 1860 and 1861: Alabama, Arkansas, Florida, Georgia, Louisiana, Mississippi, North Carolina, South Carolina, Tennessee, Texas, and Virginia.

enfranchisement—Being given the right to vote.

eulogize—To speak admiringly of someone after his or her death.

fanaticism—Extreme enthusiasm for a religion or other cause.

fraudulent—Deceptive.

Reconstruction—The process of restoring the former Confederate States to the Union after the Civil War. Lasting from 1865 to 1877, Reconstruction tried to reshape the conquered South through various efforts and to extend civil rights to the former slaves.

secede—To withdraw formally from a group or organization.

Sibyl—A mythological female prophet.

slander—Oral statements that hurt a person's reputation.

suffrage—The right to vote.

Union—The states that remained loyal to the United States during the Civil War.

Yankee—A nickname for a Union soldier.

FURTHER READING

Books

Altman, Linda Jacobs. *Slavery and Abolition in American History.* Berkeley Heights, N.J.: Enslow Publishers, Inc., 1999.

Kent, Zachary. *The Civil War: "A House Divided."* Hillside, N.J.: Enslow Publishers, Inc., 1994.

Kerby, Mona. *Frederick Douglass.* New York: Franklin Watts, Inc., 1995.

Kraus, Peter. *Sojourner Truth: Antislavery Activist.* New York: Chelsea House Publishers, 1989.

Loos, Pamela. *Elizabeth Cady Stanton: Woman Suffragist.* New York: Chelsea House Publishers, 1999.

McKissack, Patricia, and Fredrick McKissack. *Sojourner Truth: Ain't I a Woman?* New York: Scholastic, Inc., 1992.

McLoone, Margo. *Sojourner Truth.* Mankato, Minn.: Bridgestone Press, 1997.

Nash, Carol Rust. *The Fight for Women's Right to Vote in American History.* Springfield, N.J.: Enslow Publishers, Inc., 1998.

Ortiz, Victoria. *Sojourner Truth: A Self-Made Woman.* Philadelphia: J. B. Lippincott, 1974.

Whalin, Terry. *Sojourner Truth.* Uhrichsville, Ohio: Barbour and Co., 1997.

Internet Addresses

"African Americans in History." *Institute for African American Studies at the University of Georgia.* n.d. <http://www.uga.edu/~iaas/History.html> (June 29, 2000).

"Ain't I a Woman?" *Digital Sojourn.* n.d. <http://www.digitalsojourn.org/speech.html> (June 29, 2000).

Northampton Historical Society. "Honoring Sojourner Truth." *The Sojourner Truth Memorial Statue Committee.* n.d. <http://www.noho.com/sojourner/> (June 29, 2000).

"Sojourner Truth, The Libyan Sibyl." *Afro-American Almanac.* n.d. <http://www.toptags.com/aama/books/book6.htm> (June 29, 2000).

INDEX

7/04   1   3/04
2110 ⑥
11/14 ⑨
3/16 ⑪